THE TRIUMPH OF THE CLASSICAL

CAMBRIDGE ARCHITECTURE 1804–1834

FITZWILLIAM MUSEUM, CAMBRIDGE

THE TRIUMPH OF
THE CLASSICAL

CAMBRIDGE ARCHITECTURE 1804–1834

EXHIBITION CATALOGUED
WITH AN INTRODUCTION BY
DAVID WATKIN

CAMBRIDGE UNIVERSITY PRESS

CAMBRIDGE

LONDON · NEW YORK · MELBOURNE

FOR THE FITZWILLIAM MUSEUM

CAMBRIDGE

Published by the Syndics of the Cambridge University Press
The Pitt Building, Trumpington Street, Cambridge CB2 1RP
Bentley House, 200 Euston Road, London NW1 2DB
32 East 57th Street, New York, NY 10022, USA
296 Beaconsfield Parade, Middle Park, Melbourne 3206, Australia

First published 1977
Reprinted 1978

Library of Congress Cataloging in Publication Data
Watkin, David, 1941–
The triumph of the classical
At head of title: Fitzwilliam Museum, Cambridge.
Held at the Fitzwilliam Museum, Sept.–Nov. 1977.
1. Neoclassicism (Architecture) – England – Cambridge – Exhibitions.
2. Architecture, Modern – 19th century – England – Cambridge – Exhibitions.
3. Cambridge – Buildings.
I. Cambridge. University. Fitzwilliam Museum.
II. Title
NA971.C3W37   720′.9426′5907402659   77–12164
ISBN 0 521 21854 3 hard covers
ISBN 0 521 29292 1 paperback

CONTENTS

THE PLATES

LIST OF PLATES

FOREWORD

To offer Cambridge an exhibition of three Cambridge triumphs for Neo-Classicism in the early nineteenth century 'Battle of the Styles' has been for some time a cherished ambition of mine: Wilkins's Downing, Cockerell's University Library and Basevi's Fitzwilliam Museum. These triumphs were of more than local significance in their conception, in the kind of opposition which they encountered, and in their realisation. It was clear that the exhibition could best come to being in the Fitzwilliam, and with the expert guidance of my colleague in the University's Department of Architecture and History of Art, Dr David Watkin. Dr Watkin has selected the exhibits, written the catalogue, and thus put the issues and their resolution most illuminatingly in their full historical context. We are outstandingly in his debt.

On his behalf as well as the Museum's, I would like to thank those responsible for the generous loans: in Cambridge, the Master and Fellows of Trinity College, the Master and Fellows of Downing College, the Provost and Fellows of King's College, the Syndics of the University Library, and the Committee of the Cambridge Antiquarian Society; and in London, the Royal Institute of British Architects and the Victoria and Albert Museum. At the London institutions we have particular reasons to be grateful to Mr John Harris, Curator of the RIBA Drawings Collection, and to Dr C. M. Kauffman, Keeper of the Department of Paintings, Drawings and Prints at the V. & A.

A highly desirable feature of an exhibition which is substantially of architectural drawings, the provision of small-scale models in three dimensions, was made possible by a grant from the Arts Council of Great Britain. We thank the Arts Council for backing the much-to-be-appreciated work and skill of the model makers, Mr Gavin Stamp and Mr Robin Hill. We thank also the Syndics and staff of the Cambridge University Press for their sympathetic collaboration and for their decisive contribution to the production of the catalogue, itself a distinguished contribution to the literature of Neo-Classicism.

MICHAEL JAFFÉ
Director

ABBREVIATIONS

d   dated
dem   demolished
insc   inscribed
in   inch
mm   millimetre
s   signed
w/m   watermark

Unless otherwise stated the place of publication of all books
cited is London.

INTRODUCTION

The age of Neo-Classicism from the mid-eighteenth to the early-nineteenth century was the age of museums and mausolea, of libraries and universities, of belief in the instructive nobility of antique culture as evoked by Winckelmann. This tradition produced a late flowering in Cambridge in the form of the college, the library and the museum which form the core of the present exhibition.

These buildings were not only classical in new and important ways but they were also revolutionary for Cambridge in character and aim. Downing College abandoned the closed mediaeval court of the traditional Cambridge college with its celibate dons, in favour of a large and open campus-type plan incorporating houses for married professors: neither the architectural style nor the general layout has found imitators in Cambridge, an indication of their profound novelty. The University Library was a project for far more than a library: it was to be a miniature university combining lecture rooms for mathematics and the natural sciences as well as for the arts; museums for geology, mineralogy, botany and zoology; the administrative offices of the university; as well as the university library itself together with offices for the librarian and the Syndics. Had Cockerell's full scheme been executed, it would have transformed the intellectual and architectural character of the university. The Fitzwilliam Museum, too, represented a completely novel departure. The university's imaginative response to Lord Fitzwilliam's bequest has given us a dominating and unforgettable monument which, with its rich collections, vies in interest for the visitor to Cambridge with King's College Chapel itself.

The three buildings also have a stylistic as well as a functional significance. They represent three different interpretations of the classical language of architecture. In the domesticated Athenian of Wilkins's college we can all recognise something characteristically Georgian, refined and understated; Cockerell's library betrays a bolder hand, astringent, individual yet scholarly; while Basevi's museum, ebullient but never coarse, has a late Roman swagger: Balbec corrected by modern taste. The buildings were also 'programmatic' in the sense of being designed by important London architects as statements of faith in the classical revival. The relatively modest Downing established the Greek Revival and thus paved the way for Cockerell's University Library which in turn made the even more eye-catching Fitzwilliam Museum seem acceptable. All three buildings were, moreover, built by architects conscious of a threat to the survival of the classical tradition in which they had been trained. This threat was, of course, the Gothic Revival and it is perhaps not always appreciated that designs in the Gothic as well as the classical styles were submitted in the competitions for Downing College, the University Library and the Fitzwilliam Museum. Thus the Battle of the Styles, sometimes exclusively connected with the conflict between Lord Palmerston and George Gilbert Scott over the style of the Foreign Office in the 1850s, was begun in Cambridge as soon as the nineteenth century opened.

In England, unlike France, the Picturesque had always tended to subsume Neo-Classicism, and it was from the Picturesque that the Gothic Revival inherited a cast of mind which assumed that architecture ought to be literary, associational, narrative, moral. There can be no doubt that the Gothic Revival came to occupy in England the position that Neo-Classicism had enjoyed in Europe in the later eighteenth century: a general intellectual and cultural stimulus. Thus, despite the victory for the Greek Revival at Downing in 1804–6, colleges came increasingly to see themselves as essentially 'Gothic'. In Oxford the situation in the early years of the nineteenth century was very different. There the interest in 'appropriate' collegiate architecture took the form not of buildings in the Gothic Revival style but of the careful restoration and re-facing of mediaeval and later Gothic work. There was nothing to parallel the Battle of the Styles that was being fought at Cambridge. Yet it was no coincidence that the classical style was able to flourish at Cambridge in these years. It was the Neo-Classical movement, not the Gothic Revival, which first awakened Cambridge from the pleasant dreams of its long Georgian sleep. A group of travelling scholars, 'the Cambridge Hellenists',[1] helped to make Cambridge a centre of archaeological enquiry at the turn of the eighteenth century: Charles Kelsall (1782–1857); Edward Daniel Clarke (1769–1822), Fellow of Jesus College; J. M. Cripps (1780–1853); Edward Dodwell (1767–1832); John Chetwode Eustace (1762?–1815), chaplain to Lord Petre at Jesus College; John Tweddell (1769–1799), Fellow of Trinity College; William Gell (1777–1836), Fellow of Emmanuel College; and William Wilkins himself, Fellow of Gonville and Caius College. All were Cambridge men fired with an enthusiasm for the antique. Their enthusiasm took the practical form, characteristic of eighteenth-century Neo-Classicism, of first-hand exploration and travel in Greece and the Near East, of collecting antiquities and of publishing their travels and discoveries. Dr E. D. Clarke, for example, was a powerful influence in the university, a member of the first Fitzwilliam Museum Syndicate of 1816, and author of *Greek Marbles brought back from the Shores of the Euxine, Archipelago, and the Mediterranean, and deposited in the Vestibule of the Public Library of the University of Cambridge* (Cambridge, 1809). The book contains three drawings by Flaxman of the great caryatid which Clarke had himself brought back from the Inner Propylaea at Eleusis and which can be seen today at the Fitzwilliam Museum. Clarke was a friend of Charles Kelsall whose remarkable book, *Phantasm of an University* (1814), represents the quintessence of the high-minded reforming intellectualism which was characteristic of advanced Neo-Classicism. Kelsall's proposals for the sweeping architectural and academical reform of Oxford and Cambridge anticipate both the foundation of London University and of Jefferson's University of Virginia. The architectural layout of Kelsall's university, his 'Nurse of Universal Science' as he called it, was inspired by the Grand Prix projects of French architects of the later eighteenth century, but its centre was to be dominated by a building that was a combination of senate house, public library and museum. This was obviously inspired by the particular needs of Cambridge: we have seen, for example, how when Clarke presented the university with Greek works of art, no more appropriate setting could be found for them than the entrance to the already over-crowded university library.

DOWNING COLLEGE

Such was the intellectual atmosphere of Cambridge which, nurtured by the ideas of European Neo-Classicism, helped make possible the college, library and museum hailed in the present exhibition as the 'Triumph of the Classical'. William Wilkins (1778–1839) was the darling of the Cambridge Hellenists, the only one trained as an architect; and Thomas Hope (1769–1831), *éminence grise* of English Neo-Classicism, was Wilkins's mentor. When the controversy over the designs for Downing College first broke in 1804 Wilkins had executed no buildings but was well-known in Cambridge for his first-hand knowledge of ancient Greek architecture which shortly bore fruit in the form of his folio on *The Antiquities of Magna Graecia* (Cambridge, 1807). James Wyatt (1746–1813) had been mentioned as architect to Downing College as early as 1784, but the foundation of the college was delayed by protracted litigation so that the charter was not granted until 1800. Apparently dissatisfied with Wyatt's designs, the Master of Downing sent them early in 1804 to the fashionable collector, designer and patron, Thomas Hope, for his comments. Hope's reply took the form of a celebrated pamphlet called *Observations on the Plans and Elevations designed by James Wyatt, Architect, for Downing College, Cambridge, in a letter to Francis Annesley, esq., M.P.* (1804). In it he stated for the first time in this country the full revolutionary doctrines of French Neo-Classicism as enunciated in their most austere form in the pioneering works of the Abbé Laugier, *Essai sur l'Architecture* (1753) and *Observations sur l'Architecture* (1765). In practice this meant the Greek Revival as opposed to the laxer Roman classicism of Wyatt's designs. The Master in Chancery now intervened in the dispute over the architectural style of the college and called on an obscure architect called George Byfield to submit alternative designs. Sensing that Byfield's chances of success were slight, four more architects submitted designs voluntarily. These were Wilkins, who had been mentioned by name in Hope's pamphlet, Lewis Wyatt, who was James Wyatt's nephew, Francis Sandys and William Porden. Porden's designs were in the Perpendicular Gothic style, a surprising choice since it had been intended from the start that the college should be classical. The choice of the classical style seems to have been due to the intervention of George III who, as a pupil of Sir William Chambers, had particularly requested 'that it may not be a Gothic building'.[2] By 1806 the college and the Master in Chancery had rejected all the designs save those by Lewis Wyatt and William Wilkins. On the advice of three distinguished outside architects, George Dance, S. P. Cockerell and James Lewis, they finally selected the designs of Wilkins on 26 March 1806. This was a victory not only for Wilkins and the Greek Revival but also, in some sense, for Cambridge. With its plain undemonstrative ranges punctuated by scholarly Greek porticos, Downing set the pattern for public architecture once the post-Waterloo building boom got under way. However, in its early years Downing was not a success either socially or architecturally. Money and enthusiasm ran out so that in 1821, when work on the buildings ceased, less than half of Wilkins's plans had been carried out. Unfortunately, the unexecuted parts included what would have been the most dominant accents of the whole composition: the Greek Doric propylaeum at the entrance to the college from the north, and the balancing block on the south comprising chapel and library flanked by four Greek Ionic porticos. Maria Edgeworth visited Cambridge in 1813 and wrote in a letter that whereas Downing was said by Leslie Foster to resemble the Parthenon she 'was sadly disappointed. It will never bear comparison with King's College Chapel.'[3] It is interesting to note this new romantic feeling that Gothic is more thrilling than Greek. Even the architect C. R. Cockerell, trained in the Greek Revival, recorded the same disappointment on a visit to Downing in 1822. He summed up in his diary what many must have felt: 'quadrangle too wide. Buildings too sunk. like a string of sausages. miserable deficiency of architecture when Porticoes are passed.'[4]

One wonders how far the unhappy early history and relative failure of Downing as a college helped make its architectural style unacceptable in Cambridge however influential it may have been outside. The building of New Court at Trinity seems to have marked a decisive turning point at Cambridge. When Wilkins was approached for designs by the Master of Trinity, Christopher Wordsworth, in March 1821, it must presumably have been on the strength of his reputation as a classical architect at Downing, Haileybury and elsewhere. He submitted designs in Gothic as well as classic and though no specific style had been demanded by the college the Gothic designs were selected, doubtless because the Fellows considered that what Wilkins called his 'Monastic style'[5] was appropriate for college buildings. Wilkins was quick to discern and profit from this change of mood and went on to provide similar 'monastic' architecture at King's College and Corpus Christi College: indeed as early as 1823 he felt justified in 'considering Gothic architecture to be my *forte*'[6] in a letter to the Master of Trinity dated 8 May. This change of heart did not, however, preventing him from erecting in the classical style University College, London, St George's Hospital and the National Gallery in the later 1820s and 1830s.

The decision to 'go Gothic' at Trinity was thus of crucial importance for the future of collegiate architecture at Cambridge in the nineteenth century, most of which was to be Gothic for the same reason as at Trinity. The colleges were seen, romantically, as a mediaeval 'monastic' survival, whereas the university, expanding into a new world with new faculties and chairs, was seen as less tied to the past. This view led to an acceptance of the classical style for university but rarely for college buildings. It was an odd view when one takes into consideration the fact that the university does, after all, antedate the colleges, but it is not without its own poetic logic. None the less, the victory of the Gothic in the Battle of the Styles at Trinity was not a foregone conclusion. A Gothic New Court had its opponents, in particular the Bursar, Mr Judgson. Judgson was upset not merely by the building as erected, but by Wilkins's desire to destroy the celebrated lime avenue leading to it from the river Cam. In his first designs for New Court Wilkins ignored this avenue but the college forced him to shift the axis of the court so as to align its entrance with the avenue. Wilkins made this change with reluctance since it meant that the gateway would necessarily be asymmetrical to the west range of the court. The essentially classical outlook betrayed by this refusal to design empirically is an indication of how far Wilkins was from an understanding of the Picturesque, despite his sudden conversion to Gothic. Thus, not long after work on the building had begun, Judgson wrote a vehement letter of protest to the Master:

I understand that Wilkins is still anxious to bring about the Downfal [*sic*] of the Avenue on this side of the River...this avenue *most fortunately* veils the junction of the Library and new Building and gives a sort of feudal magnificence to the approach. If the Trees had not been there the latter would scarcely have been built in the Gothic style. As it is the Buildings have every disqualification for *joint exhibition*.[7]

Judgson's implication that New Court would have been built in the classical style but for the existence of an avenue to help blur the contrast between it and the Wren Library is surely surprising, but gives us some idea of the range of arguments that must have been used in debate by the Fellows. Wilkins's classical design was obviously intended to harmonise with the Wren Library at the same time as introducing elements borrowed from his own work at Downing. Thus the upper floors with their thin Greek details and shallow pediments rest incongruously on a heavy rusticated ground-floor in the Baroque manner of the Gibbs' Building at King's. In plan there would have been very little difference between this design and the Gothic one finally adopted, since New Court as erected is obviously thought out as a classical building: the rectangular Gothic windows would all be Georgian sashes if they could and their cusped heads are not expressed internally.

Just as no style was stipulated for New Court neither was any in the two great competitions for university buildings in the early nineteenth century: the University Library and the Fitzwilliam Museum. We can imagine, therefore, the apprehension with which an architect like C. R. Cockerell responded to his invitation to enter the limited competition for the University Library in 1829, since he knew that his whole professional future was dependent on the survival of the classical style of which he was an acknowledged master. Something of this urgency can be sensed in the special pleading contained in the explanatory document, dated 31 October 1829, which he submitted to the Vice-Chancellor with his designs:

It is presumed that the Grecian style is most appropriate to a classical Institution; is suited to all ages as maintaining the essential principles of beauty and magnificence in a superior degree, that it is most harmonious with the Senate House which must always be one of the principal ornaments of the university & which should in no way be sacrificed to the effect of any new building. The horizontal character of this building is also best contrasted with the perpendicular style of the King's Col? Chapel.

Of the Gothic it may be observed that its characteristic of loftiness & space render it unfit for a building of small comparative elevation & confined plan, that it is less suited to an academic building than the Grecian – that the beauty of the chef d'oeuvre near it must be greatly to the disadvantage of any attempt to apply it here & though a temporary celebrity has attached of late years to this style, it has never been esteemed in comparison with the Grecian at periods in which fine art has been cultivated, & will again probably sink into disrepute except in the restoration of the ancient monuments of the country.[8]

It is interesting to see how by this date the tradition of English Picturesque theory, with its emphasis on the importance of consulting the *genius loci*, had coloured the approach both of those who defended the classical and the Gothic camps in the Battle of the Styles. 'Monastic' Gothic was thus thought to be appropriate on visual and associational grounds for Trinity College, while classic was thought to be intellectually appropriate for a great modern library and also visually appropriate in terms of the opportunities for the painterly contrast of mass which the particular site afforded. The consideration which Cockerell gave to the problem of erecting on a cramped and crowded site new buildings markedly different in scale and style to the existing buildings, is in marked contrast to the absence of such discussion in the 1960s and 1970s when so many colleges seemed to believe that some special virtue resided in the violent contrast between old and new.

Of the four architects invited by the university to submit designs in limited competition for its new library Wilkins was already well known to Cambridge; Thomas Rickman (1776–1841) was in the process of erecting his eye-catching and extensive New Court in a fanciful Gothic taste at St John's College; Decimus Burton, though aged only twenty-nine, had achieved early fame with his elegant work in the heart of fashionable London: the Athenaeum, Constitution Arch and the Hyde Park Screen; while Cockerell was the least expected and most imaginative choice since he was still probably better known as a classical archaeologist than as a modern architect. His spectacular discoveries of fifth-century Greek sculpture at Aegina and Bassae had led to commissions for Greek Revival buildings which included the Hanover Chapel, dominating the upper regions of the newly laid-out Regent Street, and the Scottish National Monument in Edinburgh modelled, over-ambitiously, on the Parthenon itself.

Decimus Burton, less committed than Cockerell to classicism, played safe by submitting designs in both the classical and Gothic styles.[9] These are unfortunately now lost. The partnership of Rickman and Hutchinson submitted dull Greek designs but also prepared a captivating scheme in a sumptuous Decorated Gothic style. Refusing to be seduced by this extravaganza the Syndicate wisely pronounced C. R. Cockerell the winner of the competition in November 1829. However, it soon became clear that they had given inadequate consideration to the means by which the new building was to be financed. Thus great disquiet was expressed in the university both at the probable cost of executing Cockerell's library and at the destruction this would entail of the largely mediaeval buildings which occupied the site. The solution was the appointment of a second Syndicate which in June 1830 invited the same architects to submit fresh designs for a building 'in the Grecian style of architecture' capable of being erected in two phases, the first to cost not more than £25,000 and to occupy the western part of the site, i.e. the Old Court of King's College. This Syndicate complicated the issue further by selecting not Cockerell's designs but those submitted by Rickman and his partner Hutchinson. Cockerell, however, had powerful advocates in the university, in particular two Fellows of Trinity, the Rev. G. Peacock and the Rev. H. Coddington, who published four pamphlets on his behalf between 1831 and 1835. The other architects, less fortunate, tried to gain support with pamphlets of their own authorship. By November 1835 a third Syndicate had decided that the battle could only be resolved by holding yet a third competition. Once more the long-suffering architects submitted designs and on 11 May 1836 Cockerell's were selected by a large majority. However, he could not promise to keep within the £25,000 limit, so that in June 1836 demolition of the Old Court of King's was halted. A hope that some parts of the mediaeval structure could be incorporated into the new buildings was rejected by a building Syndicate in March 1837. The same Syndicate recommended that instead of proceeding with the construction of parts of the west, north and south ranges of Cockerell's library courtyard and thus involving the total demolition of the Old Court of King's, work should be limited to construction of the whole north range of the library so as to leave intact for the time being both the Old Schools courtyard and most of King's courtyard. This reasonable compromise was adopted and the foundation stone of what is now the Squire Law Library was laid on 29 September 1837. When work was finished on this building five years later at a cost of £35,000 it must have seemed fairly clear to Cockerell that this was as much of his great scheme as was ever likely to be completed.

The aloofness and austerity of the existing building are in part explained by the fact that though it was certainly to be one side of a four-sided courtyard it was also in some sense merely the flanking and recessed pavilion of a composition whose interest was centred in the great Ionic colonnade of the east entrance-front. Another moment of drama would have been the courtyard itself enclosed by richly articulated façades with engaged columns carrying a tall attic crowned with great arched chimney-stacks. Brilliantly combining elements from Greek, Late Roman, Mannerist and English Baroque architecture, and in some ways anticipating the néo-grec of mid-nineteenth-century French architecture, Cockerell's library would have been one of the most challenging and original architectural masterpieces of the century anywhere in Europe.

THE FITZWILLIAM MUSEUM

The infelicitous way in which Wyatt was dropped suddenly as architect of Downing College in favour of Wilkins and the flagrant irresponsibility characteristic of the conduct of the University Library competition, were to be echoed again and again in architectural competitions throughout the nineteenth century. Cambridge, however, seemed determined to profit by her lesson, so that the competition for the Fitzwilliam Museum, held in 1834, was managed with admirable smoothness. Richard, 7th Viscount Fitzwilliam, died in 1816, leaving his collections to the university. These were temporarily displayed in the old Perse School in Free School Lane which was adapted for the purpose by William Wilkins. A great variety of sites for a new museum was now proposed and rejected. In 1821–3 a suitable though rather narrow site was acquired from Peterhouse which was not to become out of lease until 1835. The competition, which was open and not limited like that for the University Library, was announced in July 1834. Few instructions were issued to competitors beyond a request for space, at a cost of no more than £40,000, for 200 pictures with room for possible future additions. By the closing date in November 1834 twenty-seven architects had submitted a total of

12 thirty-six designs, most of which are now lost. The 1830s was not, on the whole, a very distinguished period in English architecture and the names of those competing do not form an impressive list. Apart from Basevi, whose designs were selected by a large majority in October 1835, Pennethorne, Salvin and the ever-hopeful Wilkins were the only architects of any distinction. Cockerell did not compete: presumably the chaotic handling of the Library competition had acted as a powerful dissuasion. George Basevi (1794–1845), a refined and scholarly pupil of Soane, never had a large practice and would have been best-known for his town-planning in London which included the designing of Belgrave Square.

The year of the Fitzwilliam Museum competition, 1834, was also the year of the celebrated fire at the Houses of Parliament. In 1835 it was decided to seek designs for new Houses of Parliament 'in the Gothic or Elizabethan style'. First it had been colleges that were to be designed in the Gothic style on largely spurious associational grounds; now the chambers of legislature were to be decked in similar garb on national grounds. It was felt that the essentially English nature of the two Houses of Parliament was best expressed and upheld in an essentially English style, 'Elizabethan', as opposed to Neo-Classicism which was increasingly seen as alien and cosmopolitan. Could it be, thought Rickman and Hussey, that museums would be the next to fall before the onslaught of 'associationism'? Thus, along with their classical proposals for the Fitzwilliam they submitted a set of spectacular Gothic designs. In fact they were only twenty years too soon, for the first Gothic museum of the nineteenth century was Deane and Woodward's Oxford Museum of 1855. There is thus a sense in which Rickman and Hussey were nearer to reality than Cockerell with his wishful thinking of 1829 that the Gothic 'will again probably sink into disrepute except in the restoration of the ancient monuments of the country'.

Basevi's magnificent design was characteristically Neo-Classical in its reliance on the fruits of recent archaeological discovery; but where Wilkins at Downing and Cockerell at the University Library had drawn on Greek sources – the Erechtheion and the Temple of Apollo at Bassae respectively – Basevi looked to a Roman building, the grandiose Capitolium at Brescia which had been excavated in 1820. From this he seems to have derived the theme of extending the portico into the side wings in the form of a colonnade. Like the great terminal pylons or pavilions of the main façade, this device was adopted to help distract attention from the fact that the extreme narrowness of Trumpington Street made it impossible to obtain a central axial view of the portico. At the same time he had a proto-Victorian ambition for his building to be dominant, colourful and eye-catching, since he must have realised that if the classical tradition was to survive in modern England it would have to capture something of the immediate dramatic appeal present in Rickman and Hussey's Gothic designs. Thus on the site plan that he submitted with his designs he explained that he had chosen a square rather than a longer and narrower plan 'because a wider space is gained on each side, and the building is sufficiently detached to be well seen not in groupe [*sic*] with other and meaner buildings but *by itself* – a point of primary importance in street architecture'. He claimed that 'For the same reason, the floor of the Portico is elevated upon a high platform and the steps are brought to the line of the pavement that the Edifice may not appear to lose size in the perspective from other objects being more immediately in the foreground.' Trained, as he was, in the Neo-Classical tradition his mind naturally sought parallels in the architecture of Greece and Rome. He thus argued that:

the effect of the Portico of the Pantheon at Rome is injured by its present low position and the vicinity of the other buildings – and on the contrary how finely the detached and elevated situation of the Greek temples accords with their symmetry – in some places crowning an Acropolis – in others occupying a rising ground, and always standing on a high platform.[10]

Work on Basevi's museum was begun in 1837 and the structure was complete by 1844, in which year he was instructed to begin work on the interior. After his tragic fall to his death at Ely Cathedral in 1845, the Syndicate wisely appointed as his successor C. R. Cockerell, who had

14 gained the confidence of the university during the construction of the University Library. It was also a happy choice from an artistic point of view since he and Basevi shared common stylistic aims. In the galleries Cockerell carried out faithfully Basevi's decorative intentions in plasterwork of astonishing beauty but in the staircase-hall, the design of which Basevi had himself altered more than once, Cockerell introduced a greater richness of effect. However, money ran out in 1847 and the staircase-hall was left in an uncompleted state for nearly a quarter of a century. Then in the palmy 1870s the architect E. M. Barry wondrously transformed the whole space by unleashing into it a rich cascade of sumptuous marbles, a molten polychromy of chocolate, ox-blood and amber, which overnight provided the museum with one of the most powerfully eloquent statements of High Victorian classicism in the country. The modulation of Basevi's comparatively chaste Neo-Classical hall into, firstly, Cockerell's more richly articulated design and finally into Barry's extravagantly exuberant showpiece, echoes the changing interpretations of the antique which we have seen exemplified in the development from Wilkins's Downing through Cockerell's library to Basevi's museum: the development we have characterised as the 'Triumph of the Classical'.

NOTES

1 For a fuller discussion of the Cambridge Hellenists and of Kelsall in particular, see my *Thomas Hope (1769–1831) and the Neo-Classical Idea*, 1968, chap. 3, and 'Charles Kelsall: the Quintessence of Neo-Classicism', *Architectural Review*, CXL, August 1966, 109–12.
2 Quoted in a letter from Michael Lort, Fellow of Trinity College, dated 27 October 1784 (R. Willis & J. W. Clarke, *Architectural History of the University of Cambridge*, 4 vols., Cambridge 1886–7, vol. 2, pp. 756–7).
3 *Life and Letters of Maria Edgeworth*, ed. A. J. C. Hare, 1894, p. 178.
4 D. J. Watkin, *The Life and Work of C. R. Cockerell, R.A.*, 1974, p. 69.
5 In a letter to the Master of Trinity College, dated 6 June 1821 (in a MS. volume entitled *Building of the New Court, 1821–1830*, fo. 40, Trinity College archives).

6 In a letter to the Master of Trinity College, dated 8 May 1823 (*Building of the New Court, 1821–1830*, fo. 44).

7 In a letter to the Master of Trinity College, dated 9 December, no year but w/m is 1823 (*Building of the New Court, 1821–1830*, fo. 290).

8 Cambridge University Library, Add. MS. 6630.

9 According to some comments in Rickman's diary quoted in A. James, 'Rickman and the Fitzwilliam Competition', *Architectural Review*, CXXI, April 1957, 270.

10 Quoted from notes on Basevi's site plan preserved with his other competition drawings of 1834 in the Fitzwilliam Museum Library.

DOWNING COLLEGE

James Wyatt had been mentioned as architect of Downing as early as 1784. The three surviving designs by him exhibited here may date from that period. In 1800 the college received its charter after years of litigation; and at the beginning of 1804 the Master of Downing sent Wyatt's designs to the Neo-Classical pundit, Thomas Hope, for his opinion. Hope's reply took the form of a celebrated pamphlet, dated 22 February 1804, which was a classic and influential statement of the Greek Revival as against the tired Palladianism of the eighteenth century. Its immediate consequence was that George Byfield was invited to submit alternative designs to Wyatt's. In 1805 four other architects decided of their own accord to join in the fray: these included Porden, whose designs were in a fanciful and elaborate Gothic style, and Wilkins, Hope's protégé, whose Greek Revival designs adopted all the recommendations made in Hope's pamphlet. The college finally selected Wilkins's designs in 1806 and his east and west ranges were erected from 1807 to 1821. His north and south ranges, the high points of his whole composition, have unfortunately never been executed.

1 JAMES WYATT (1746–1813)

Design for Downing College, Cambridge
Perspective from the SW
Pen and wash within ruled border: 250×650 mm ($9\frac{7}{8} \times 25\frac{1}{2}$ in); s: James Wyatt Archt
EXHIBITED: 'The Age of Neo-Classicism', London, 1972.
REPRODUCED: G. Walkley, 'Designs for Downing College, Cambridge', *RIBA Journal*, XLV, 1938, 1014; A. Dale, *James Wyatt*, Oxford 1956, pl. 41; J. M. Crook, *Haileybury and the Greek Revival: the Architecture of William Wilkins, RA*, Hoddesdon 1964, p. 10; *Catalogue of the Drawings Collection of the RIBA, The Wyatt Family*, 1973, fig. 29
LITERATURE: T. Hope, *Observations on the Plans...by James Wyatt*

Lent by the RIBA Drawings Collection

This and the two following designs are for a quadrangle 250 feet
square with the S range extended to E and W so as to project beyond
the quadrangle proper. The chapel was in the middle of this long S
range with a four-columned Roman Doric portico on both its N and S
fronts. The quadrangle was entered from a triumphal arch in the middle
of the N range and there were side entrances flanked by columns in
antis in the middle of the E and W ranges. The round-headed windows on
either side of the portico on the S front seem to echo those at Wren's
Chelsea Hospital, but the triumphal archway resembles Wyatt's gateway at Canterbury Quad, Christ Church, Oxford (1773–83), and the side
entrances recall the W front of his Dodington Park, Avon (1798–1808).
The most interesting feature was the square tower over the chapel
adorned with columns in antis and sunken corner-panels and surmounted
by a shallow, domed octagonal cupola. But the composition of the college
as a whole was tired, lumpish and arbitrarily articulated, an easy prey
for Hope's waspish pen.

2   JAMES WYATT (1746–1813)
Design for Downing College, Cambridge
Perspective from the NW
Pen and wash within ruled border: 250×645 mm ($9\frac{7}{8} \times 25\frac{3}{8}$ in); s: James
    Wyatt Archt
REPRODUCED: G. Walkley, 'Designs for Downing College, Cambridge',
    RIBA Journal, XLV, 1938, 1015; *Catalogue of the Drawings Collection
    of the RIBA, The Wyatt Family,* 1973, fig. 30
EXHIBITED: 'The Age of Neo-Classicism', London, 1972
Lent by the RIBA Drawings Collection

18 This view shows the entrance gateway in the form of a triumphal arch in the centre of the N range.

3 JAMES WYATT (1746–1813)
Design for Downing College, Cambridge
Perspective of the courtyard looking S
Pen and wash within ruled border: 320×785 mm ($12\frac{1}{2} \times 31$ in)
REPRODUCED: J. M. Crook, *The Greek Revival*, RIBA Drawings Series, 1968, pl. 14; *Catalogue of the Drawings Collection of the RIBA, The Wyatt Family*, 1973, fig. 31
EXHIBITED: 'The Age of Neo-Classicism', London, 1972
Lent by the RIBA Drawings Collection

The continuous Roman Doric colonnade surrounding the courtyard represents Wyatt's response to Neo-Classical stylophily. Though eye-catching in a watercolour (note the thunderous sky), it would have been both expensive to construct and deeply depressing in its effect on the rooms which lay behind it.

4 WILLIAM PORDEN (*c.* 1755–1822)
Design for Downing College, Cambridge, 1805
Plan
Pen and wash within ruled border: w/m 1804: 525×650 mm ($20\frac{3}{4} \times 25\frac{1}{2}$ in); over the central block is a flier (355×250 mm: $14 \times 9\frac{7}{8}$ in) showing an alternative plan
LITERATURE: A. Dale, *James Wyatt*, Oxford 1956, p. 90; *Catalogue of the Drawings Collection of the RIBA, O–R*, 1976, pp. 90–1
Lent by the RIBA Drawings Collection

Porden, a former pupil of Wyatt's, was one of four architects who submitted designs for Downing College voluntarily in 1805 when it became clear that James Wyatt's chances of final victory were slight. Porden's own architectural practice was neither distinguished nor extensive, but his elaborately Perpendicular Gothic Eaton Hall for Lord Grosvenor of 1804 had won him a certain notoriety. The plan and three elevations for Downing now on exhibition have been chosen from thirty drawings by him for the college in the Gothic style which survive in the RIBA Drawings Collection. The detailed effort he put into his scheme represents a great statement of faith in the Gothic Revival, since it had been intended from the start (following a wish expressed by George III) that the college would be built in the classical style.

5 WILLIAM PORDEN (*c.* 1755–1822)
Design for Downing College, Cambridge, 1805
N front
Pen and watercolour within double ruled border: w/m 1804: 340 × 675 mm (13⅜ × 26½ in); s: W. Porden, Architect
REPRODUCED: *Catalogue of the RIBA Drawings Collection, O–R*, 1976, fig. 39
Lent by the RIBA Drawings Collection

6 WILLIAM PORDEN (*c.* 1755–1822)   PLATE **3**
Design for Downing College, Cambridge, 1805
S front
Pen and watercolour within double ruled border: 340 × 530 mm (13⅜ × 20⅞ in); s: as for no. 5
Lent by the RIBA Drawings Collection

In the centre is the apsed S (liturgical E) end of the chapel flanked on the left by the Combination Room and on the right by the Reading Room. The huge Combination Room, resembling the choir of some great Gothic church, would have been a striking departure from Cambridge precedent. The elevation corresponds with the original plan, not with that on the flier of no. 4.

7 WILLIAM PORDEN (*c.* 1755–1822)

Design for Downing College, Cambridge, 1805

E front

Pen and watercolour within double ruled border: w/m 1804: 340 × 675 mm ($13\frac{3}{8}$ × $26\frac{1}{2}$ in); s: as for no. 5

Lent by the RIBA Drawings Collection

8 GEORGE BYFIELD (*c.* 1756–1813)

Design for Downing College, Cambridge, 1804

Site plan

Pen, partly tinted, within double ruled border: 455 × 685 mm (18 × $26\frac{7}{8}$ in) s and d: G. Byfield Craven St. 1804

Lent by the Master and Fellows, Downing College, Cambridge

9 GEORGE BYFIELD (*c.* 1756–1813)

Design for Downing College, Cambridge, 1804

Section from N to S; E elevation of E and W fronts

Watercolour within single ruled border: 490 × 920 mm ($19\frac{1}{4}$ × $36\frac{1}{4}$ in); s and d: as for no. 8

Lent by the Master and Fellows, Downing College, Cambridge

10 LEWIS WILLIAM WYATT (1777–1853)

Design for Downing College, Cambridge, 1805

Ground-floor plan

Pen and pencil within single ruled border: 615 × 735 mm ($24\frac{1}{4}$ × 29 in); s and d: Lewis Wyatt Archt. Dec. 9. 1805

Lent by the Master and Fellows, Downing College, Cambridge

11 LEWIS WILLIAM WYATT (1777–1853)

Design for Downing College, Cambridge, 1805
Elevation of N front
Ink, partly tinted: 350 × 1160 mm (13⅞ × 45¾ in); s and d: as for no. 10.
Lent by the Master and Fellows, Downing College, Cambridge

In this rather weak composition in a tired mid-Georgian style interest
centres on a cut-down triumphal archway surmounted by a clock-turret.

12 LEWIS WILLIAM WYATT (1777–1853)   PLATE 2

Design for Downing College, Cambridge, 1805
Elevation of S front
Watercolour: 360 × 1160 mm (14¼ × 45¾ in); s and d: as for no. 10
EXHIBITED: 'The Age of Neo-Classicism', London, 1972
REPRODUCED: B. Little, 'Cambridge and the Campus', *Virginia Maga-
zine of History and Biography*, LXXIX, April 1971, 190–201
Lent by the Master and Fellows, Downing College, Cambridge

This powerful watercolour with its dark sky shows the most memorable
part of Wyatt's design, the S front of the S range of the courtyard, and
enables us to understand why it survived in the competition longer than
those by Byfield, Sandys and Porden. Untouched by the Greek Revival,
the design is in the style of a quarter of a century earlier and can be com-
pared with the garden-front of A. Rousseau's Hôtel de Salm, Paris
(1784). The central domed rotunda contained the apse of the chapel
with the altar placed on the chord. A sectional drawing, preserved in the
college, shows that the interior of this splendid chapel would have been
adorned with plasterwork in a manner inspired by the architect's uncle,
James Wyatt.

13 WILLIAM WILKINS (1778–1839)

Design for Downing College, Cambridge
Site plan
Pen, partly tinted: 350 × 465 mm (13¾ × 18⅜ in)
Lent by the Master and Fellows, Downing College, Cambridge

This interesting plan shows clearly the relation of the Greek Doric propylaea to the court and also to the road of terraced houses with which it was proposed to connect the court and Pembroke Street. An alternative plan, mounted in the same album, shows a more dramatic and impractical arrangement with the propylaea isolated from the college and placed in Pembroke Street at the N end of the terraced houses.

14 WILLIAM WILKINS (1778–1839)

Design for Downing College, Cambridge
Perspective of S front
Watercolour within lined border: 495 × 1790 mm (19½ × 70½ in)
EXHIBITED: 'The Age of Neo-Classicism', London, 1972
REPRODUCED: B. Little, 'Cambridge and the Campus', *Virginia Magazine of History and Biography*, LXXIX, April 1971, 190–201.
Lent by the Master and Fellows, Downing College, Cambridge

15 WILLIAM WILKINS (1778–1839)

Design for Downing College, Cambridge
Perspective from the SW
Pen and watercolour: 350 × 740 mm (13¾ × 29¼ in); s and d: J. Bailey 1830
Lent by the Master and Fellows, Downing College, Cambridge

16 WILLIAM WILKINS (1778–1839)
Design for Downing College, Cambridge
Ground-floor plan of library and chapel
Pen, partly tinted: 460 × 920 mm (18 × 36⅛ in)
Lent by the Master and Fellows, Downing College, Cambridge

Control of interior space seems not to have been Wilkins's *forte*, as can be
seen from the way in which the visitor, having entered the building
through the centre of the portico, would find himself near the edge and
not in the centre of the entrance hall.

17 WILLIAM WILKINS (1778–1839)
Design for Downing College, Cambridge
N elevation of the propylaea
Pen and pencil, partly tinted: 460 × 925 mm (18⅛ × 36⅜ in)
REPRODUCED: D. J. Watkin, *Thomas Hope (1769–1831) and the Neo-
Classical Idea*, 1968, pl. 17
Lent by the Master and Fellows, Downing College, Cambridge

This is one of the central designs of British Neo-Classical architecture.
The first measured drawings of the propylaea, gateway to the Athenian
Acropolis, were published in Stuart and Revett's *Antiquities of Athens*,
vol. 2, 1789, the first building inspired by it was Langhans's Branden-
burg Gate in Berlin (1789–93) and the second Harrison's Chester Castle
gateway of *c*. 1810. Note Wilkins's careful instructions on this working
drawing as to the correct laying of stones: 'The Epistylea [architraves]
must be single stones in length they may be two stones in width. The
tympanum of the pediment to have no horizontal joints.'

24 18 WILLIAM WILKINS (1778–1839)
Design for Downing College, Cambridge
Ground-floor plan of hall
Ink, partly tinted: 470 × 685 mm (18½ × 27 in); s: William Wilkins
Archt. Feby. 1818
Lent by the Master and Fellows, Downing College, Cambridge

This drawing shows the unhappy way in which the single temple-like
pavilion was divided internally so as to form a Combination Room at
the W end. In 1969 the partition wall was removed and the whole building
sympathetically restored so as to allow the hall to fill the entire space.

TRINITY COLLEGE

Wilkins was invited in March 1821 by the Master of Trinity, Christopher Wordsworth, to submit plans for a new court. Wilkins submitted designs in the classical and Gothic styles. The latter were eventually selected; the building was begun in 1823 and occupied in 1825. The decision to adopt what Wilkins called 'the Monastic style' had a great influence on college building in the nineteenth century.

19 WILLIAM WILKINS (1778–1839)   PLATE 4
Design for New Court, Trinity College, Cambridge, 1821
Elevation showing W front of proposed new court in relation to the W
   front of the Wren Library
Pen and watercolour: 465 × 915 mm (18¾ × 36 in)
Lent by the Master and Fellows of Trinity College, Cambridge

Wilkins's aim in preparing this view must have been to convince the Fellows of Trinity that his designs for New Court in the classical style would have harmonised with the Wren Library. Thus, although the upper storeys of New Court are in a chaste Greek Revival style the rusticated ground floor has a Baroque emphasis.

THE OBSERVATORY

A building syndicate for a new observatory on a site north of the Madingley Road was appointed in 1820. In October 1821 architects were invited to submit designs by 1 January 1822. Thirteen sent in designs. Those by J. C. Mead were awarded the first prize, the second prize going to Wilkins. So far as we know, none of the designs was in the Gothic style. (This is in striking contrast to the limited competition held in 1828 for the Pitt Press in Trumpington Street, since the Press Syndicate seems to have decided at an early stage, for reasons that are unclear, that the Press should be Gothic.) Construction of the Observatory was begun in 1822 and was completed the following year at a cost of £16,340.

20 JOHN CLEMENT MEAD (1798–1831)
Design for the Cambridge Observatory, 1821
Perspective from the SE
Pen and watercolour: 630 × 1240 mm (24⅝ × 48⅝ in)
LITERATURE: R. Willis & J. W. Clark, *Architectural History of the University of Cambridge*, 4 vols., Cambridge 1886–7, vol. 3, pp. 224–9
Lent by the Institute of Astronomy, University of Cambridge

In 1820 Mead obtained the second premium in the important competition for the New General Post Office in London at the remarkably early age of twenty-two. This must have given him confidence in entering the Observatory competition, and it must have been galling for Wilkins to be defeated in his own university by a man twenty years his junior. Mead's winning design has many peculiarities and refinements of detail which repay study and which suggest he had studied the work of Sir John Soane. The composition of the side façades flanking the central portico, based on the Doric order of the Parthenon, is distinctly odd and has an unexpected almost Mannerist rhythm. These façades are

elaborately articulated with horizontally channelled rustication and with
the full triglyph frieze of the Doric order except in the end bays where
their omission is presumably intended to emphasise the domestic character of the extremities of the building which contained houses for the
Observer and Deputy Observer. The frieze is related not to columns but
to oddly paced anta-strips which support in a Soaneic manner segmental
lugs above the cornice.

21 RICHARD BANKS HARRADEN (1778–1862)   PLATE 5
Cambridge from the Observatory, *c.* 1823
Oil on canvas: 700 × 1030 mm (27½ × 40½ in)
Lent anonymously

This romantic view, in which the Greek Observatory and the Gothic
King's College Chapel balance each other across a Claudian landscape,
might almost have been painted to convert to the Greek Revival the
novelist Maria Edgeworth who, having been told that Downing College
resembled the Parthenon, complained on visiting the college that it
would never bear comparison with King's College Chapel (see Introduction, p. 5).

KING'S COLLEGE

Proposals for completing the great court of King's, of which one side was taken up by the chapel and the other by the Gibbs' Building, were made by Robert Adam in 1784 in the classical style and by James Wyatt in 1795 in the Gothic style. Wyatt's drawing establishes the theme of a low screen along the street front so as to close the court without obscuring the chapel. Not until 1822 did the college finally decide to bring its court to a conclusion. Accordingly in March of that year it advertised in the principal newspapers for designs to be submitted by October 1822 (the date was later changed to 1 January 1823). There were to be prizes for the three best designs. On 25 March 1823 those by Wilkins were awarded first prize, by W. S. Inman second prize and by Edward Lapidge third prize. Lapidge's designs were in the classical style, so that by placing them third after Gothic designs by Wilkins and by Inman, the college delivered a blow to the classical tradition. Indeed, so confident was the college that Gothic had an unchallengeable authority as the only 'collegiate' style, that it accepted Wilkins's lamentable proposals for Gothicising the Gibbs' Building. For reasons that are not recorded this Gothicisation was fortunately not carried out.

22 **EDWARD LAPIDGE** (1796–1860)
Design for King's College, Cambridge, 1822
Elevation to Trumpington Street
Ink and wash within ruled border: w/m 1801: 605 × 920 mm ($23\frac{7}{8}$ × $36\frac{1}{4}$ in); monogram: In hoc signo vinces
REPRODUCED: [J. Saltmarsh], 'King's College, Cambridge in the Making', *The Architect and Building News*, CXXXIV, 23 June 1933, repr. p. 343
Lent by the Provost and Fellows, King's College, Cambridge

A minor and not specially talented architect, Lapidge was none the less
placed third in the King's competition and was amongst the four
architects finally considered by the Senate for the Fitzwilliam Museum
in 1835. In this design for King's he produces an interesting combination of a Gibbs/Hawksmoor style with Neo-Classicism.

23 EDWARD LAPIDGE (1796–1860)   PLATE 6
Design for King's College, Cambridge, 1822
Perspective of court looking S
Ink and wash within ruled borders: 605 × 1085 mm $(23\frac{7}{8} \times 42\frac{3}{4}$ in);
    monogram: as for no. 22
Lent by the Provost and Fellows, King's College, Cambridge

On the left is the W face of the Trumpington Street (i.e. King's Parade)
front with the triumphal arch in the centre. On the right is the Gibbs'
Building 'improved' with a smart Corinthian portico.

24 ANON.
Design for King's College, Cambridge, 1822
Elevation to Trumpington Street
Pencil and wash within ruled borders: w/m 1820: 580 × 875 mm $(22\frac{3}{4} \times$
    $34\frac{1}{2}$ in)
REPRODUCED: [J. Saltmarsh], 'King's College, Cambridge in the
    Making', *The Architect and Building News*, CXXXIV, 23 June 1933,
    repr. p. 343
Lent by the Provost and Fellows, King's College, Cambridge

This anonymous design from the 1822–3 competition shows how weak
the classical style could be at this date. Even the Roman Doric triumphal arch appears bald and listless.

25 ANON.

Design for King's College, Cambridge, 1822

Perspective of court looking S

Pencil and wash within ruled borders: w/m 1820: 580 × 875 mm (22¾ × 34½ in)

Lent by the Provost and Fellows, King's College, Cambridge

Unlike Lapidge, this anonymous architect had the good sense to leave the Gibbs' Building (on the right in this view) intact. Indeed he produced a variant of it on the S side of his court.

THE UNIVERSITY LIBRARY

In a century noted for scandalously ill-conducted competitions that for the Cambridge University Library was one of the earliest and one of the most notable. The urgent need to expand the premises occupied by the university library and the university lecture-rooms had been recognised as early as 1614, and architectural solutions of the problem were regularly proposed and dismissed during the next three centuries. This long-standing game played between dons and architects about what to do with the Old Schools site came to a head in 1829 with the purchase by the university of the immediately adjacent Old Court of King's College, no longer required by King's with the completion of their new buildings by Wilkins. In the same year a limited competition for a new University Library was announced. Of the four architects invited to submit designs – two of whom sent in Gothic as well as classical designs – C. R. Cockerell was chosen in November 1829. His expensive scheme, involving demolition of the whole of the Old Schools and of the Old Court of King's, aroused much opposition in the university. Thus in 1830 a second competition was held in which the designs of Rickman and Hutchinson were selected, perhaps with a view to causing rather than resolving confusion. All parties retired to lick their wounds for five years until in 1835 a third competition was announced. Cockerell now emerged as victor, and, after much further discussion, work was begun in 1837 on the erection of the north range of his courtyard. It must have become clear fairly soon that funds and enthusiasm would be inadequate to justify continuation with the rest of his scheme. His north range survives as a poignant, isolated fragment in a characteristically English palimpsest of fortuitously preserved mediaeval, Georgian and Gothic Revival buildings.

26 THOMAS RICKMAN (1776–1841) and **HENRY HUTCHINSON** (c. 1800–1831)   PLATE 7
Competition design for University Library, Cambridge, 1829

32 Perspective from the SE (Design A with Greek Ionic order)
Pencil and wash: w/m 1827: 645 × 1075 mm (25⅜ × 42¼ in)
LITERATURE: *Catalogue of the Drawings Collection of the RIBA, O–R,*
    1976, p. 144
Lent by the RIBA Drawings Collection

This low limp design in Greek Ionic suggests that the real sympathies
of its architects lay elsewhere, in fact in the Gothic Revival. In 1817
Rickman had published his pioneering and influential study, *An Attempt
to Discriminate the Styles of English Architecture from the Conquest to the
Reformation.* He and his partner, Hutchinson, competed unsuccessfully
for the new buildings at King's College, Cambridge, in 1823, and success-
fully in 1825–6 for the New Court at St John's College, Cambridge.

**27 THOMAS RICKMAN (1776–1841) and HENRY
      HUTCHINSON (*c.* 1800–1831)**
Competition design for University Library, Cambridge, 1829
Perspective from the SW (Design A with Greek Ionic order)
Pencil and wash: w/m 1827: 650 × 1060 mm (25½ × 41¾ in)
LITERATURE: As for no. 26
Lent by the RIBA Drawings Collection

**28 THOMAS RICKMAN (1776–1841) and HENRY
      HUTCHINSON (*c.* 1800–1831)**   PLATE 8
Competition design for University Library, Cambridge, 1829
Perspective from the SE (Design B in Decorated Gothic)
Pencil and wash: 330 × 535 mm (13 × 21 in); s: TR (in monogram)
LITERATURE: As for no. 26
Lent by the RIBA Drawings Collection

Other versions of this and the next design also survive in the larger linen-backed format of nos. 26 and 27 above. The linen-backed drawings are probably those exhibited in the competition while the smaller versions, exhibited here, may possibly have been prepared for engraving. The Gothic library is undoubtedly far more eye-catching than the Greek. Its richness of effect may owe something to James Murphy's important book, *Plans, Elevations, Sections and Views of the Church of Batalha... in Portugal*, 1795. The Library Syndics were not seduced by the high drama of Rickman's designs and in the second competition held in 1830 stipulated that entries must be in 'the Grecian style of architecture'.

29 THOMAS RICKMAN (1776–1841) and **HENRY HUTCHINSON** (*c.* 1800–1831)
Competition design for University Library, Cambridge, 1829
Perspective from the SW (Design B in Decorated Gothic)
Pencil and wash: 405 × 600 mm (16 × 23$\frac{1}{2}$ in) s: *TR* (in monogram)
LITERATURE: As for no. 26
Lent by the RIBA Drawings Collection

30 WILLIAM WILKINS (1778–1839)   PLATE 9
Competition design for University Library, Cambridge
Perspective from the SE
Pencil and wash: 370 × 620 mm (14$\frac{1}{2}$ × 24$\frac{1}{2}$ in)
Lent by the University Library, Cambridge

This drawing, together with thirteen other related drawings for the library, mostly signed and dated 'William Wilkins 1830', is mounted into an album bearing a contemporary label, '*Designs for the Public Library at Cambridge*'. The drawing exhibited presumably dates from the second competition of 1830. The grotesque skyline with its conically-turreted belvederes containing figures like weathermen, looks like an afterthought intended to capture the imagination of a jaded Syndicate. Wilkins eliminated it from engraved versions of this design. The costly decastyle Corinthian portico, offspring of the one he was executing at University College, London, was intended to harmonise with the Senate House. This explains the prominent emphasis given to the latter building in Wilkins's perspective view.

31 CHARLES ROBERT COCKERELL (1788–1863)
Competition design for University Library, Cambridge
Perspective from the SE
Pencil and wash: 215 × 445 mm ($8\frac{1}{2}$ × $17\frac{1}{2}$ in); insc: no. 8 South East view
LITERATURE: D. J. Watkin, *The Life and Work of C. R. Cockerell, R. A.*, 1974, chap. 11; J. M. Crook, *The Greek Revival*, 1972, repr. pl. 187
Lent by the Victoria and Albert Museum, London

No drawings by Cockerell survive from the first competition of 1829 although this drawing, apparently dating from 1830, is for a building very similar to what we know of Cockerell's entry in the first competition. A Greek Ionic colonnade, inspired by Inigo Jones's portico at Old St Paul's Cathedral, supports a pedimented attic and is flanked by domed side-pavilions.

32 CHARLES ROBERT COCKERELL (1788–1863)
Competition design for University Library, Cambridge, 1830
View of E front
Pencil and watercolour: 559 × 940 mm (22 × 37 in); insc: no. 13; d: 9 October 1830
EXHIBITED: 'The Age of Neo-Classicism', London, 1972
REPRODUCED: J. M. Crook, *The Greek Revival*, 1972, pl. 185; *The Age of Neo-Classicism*, Catalogue, pl. 115; D. J. Watkin, *The Life and Work of C. R. Cockerell, R.A.*, 1974, pl. 85
Lent by the Victoria and Albert Museum, London

Cockerell's design in this, the second competition, replaces the colonnade 35
which characterised his designs for the first competition with an impressive portico which contains the main staircase and through which there is a view of the courtyard within. The unusual combination of a minor Greek Doric order with a major Roman Corinthian order reappeared in his unexecuted project for the Royal Exchange of 1839.

33 CHARLES ROBERT COCKERELL (1788–1863)
Competition design for University Library, Cambridge, 1830
Ground-floor plan
Reproduced from G. Peacock, *Observations on the Plans for the New Library &c. by a member of the First Syndicate*, Cambridge 1831
REPRODUCED: D. J. Watkin, *The Life and Work of C. R. Cockerell, R.A.*, 1974, pl. 83

This plan clarifies the arrangement of the double portico seen in elevation in no. 32. The staircase was inspired by seventeenth-century Italian precedent such as Longhena's at S. Giorgio Maggiore, Venice, and Bianco's at Genoa University. Schinkel's Altes Museum in Berlin of 1822 may also have served as a source.

34 CHARLES ROBERT COCKERELL (1788–1863) PLATE 11
Competition design for University Library, Cambridge, 1830
Interior of domed first-floor vestibule at junction of S and E ranges
Pencil and wash: 395×425 mm ($15\frac{1}{2} \times 16\frac{3}{4}$ in); insc: no. 12 View of the library
REPRODUCED: J. M. Crook, *The Greek Revival*, 1972, pl. 188; D. J. Watkin, *The Life and Work of C. R. Cockerell, R.A.*, 1974, pl. 86
Lent by the Victoria and Albert Museum, London

The circular vestibule owes much to Italian Renaissance design: for example Sanmicheli's Cappella Pellegrini at S. Bernardino, Verona, or

36 Palladio's chapel at Maser. The barrel-vault of the library seen through a screen of columns is an echo of the Baths of ancient Rome. There would have been a corresponding domed vestibule at the junction of the E and N ranges.

35   CHARLES ROBERT COCKERELL (1788–1863)

Competition design for University Library, Cambridge, 1830
Interior of Divinity and Law Schools
Pencil and wash: 335×390 mm ($13\frac{1}{8} \times 15\frac{1}{4}$ in); insc: no. 11 View of the
   Divinity School, also of the Law School
REPRODUCED: D. J. Watkin, *The Life and Work of C. R. Cockerell, R.A.*,
   1974, pl. 87
Lent by the Victoria and Albert Museum, London

The Divinity School and the Law School were identically designed lecture-rooms occupying most of the ground floor of the S range of the courtyard. These subjects had been taught on this site from the fourteenth century onwards and it was an essential part of Cockerell's programme to provide the necessary lecture-rooms. The Greek Doric columns are of lead-bearing stone and support iron beams which in turn carry the iron cores of the wood-encased columns in the first-floor libraries (see no. 34).

36   CHARLES ROBERT COCKERELL (1788–1863)

Competition design for University Library, Cambridge
Ground-floor plan with E and W elevations
Pen, partly tinted: 405×860 mm ($16 \times 33\frac{3}{4}$ in)
REPRODUCED: D. J. Watkin, *The Life and Work of C. R. Cockerell, R.A.*,
   1974, pl. 88
Lent by the Victoria and Albert Museum, London

Like the remainder of the drawings exhibited, this plan seems to belong
to the third competition of 1835–6. The plan of the N range (along the
bottom of the drawing) is still not quite that of the building executed,
and the elevations appended to the plan lack the powerful arched motif
of the executed building.

37 CHARLES ROBERT COCKERELL (1788–1863)
Competition design for University Library, Cambridge
E elevation
Pencil, partly tinted; tracing: w/m 1834: 230 × 700 mm (9 × 27$\frac{1}{2}$ in)

Like the following drawing this elevation relates to those appended to
the plan in no. 36.

38 CHARLES ROBERT COCKERELL (1788–1863)
Competition design for University Library, Cambridge
S elevation
Pencil, partly tinted; tracing: w/m 1834: 235 × 865 mm (9$\frac{1}{4}$ × 34 in)

39 CHARLES ROBERT COCKERELL (1788–1863)
Competition design for University Library, Cambridge
W elevation, with part plan; *verso:* perspective sketch showing windows
  in courtyard
Pencil, partly tinted: 295 × 675 mm (11$\frac{5}{8}$ × 26$\frac{1}{2}$ in)
LITERATURE: D. J. Watkin, *The Life and Work of C. R. Cockerell, R.A.*,
  1974, chap. 11, repr. pl. 91
Lent by the Victoria and Albert Museum, London

This highly original composition might be considered rather overpower-
ing for its constricted site in Trinity Hall Lane, but the open space in
front of Clare College would have been opposite its more important
right-hand, or southern, half. Unlike the three previous drawings (nos.

36–8) this introduces the motif of an arched window breaking into an attic which was adopted for the E front of the wing eventually executed.

40 CHARLES ROBERT COCKERELL (1788–1863)

PLATE 10

Competition design for University Library, Cambridge
Elevation of W side of courtyard
Pencil, partly tinted: 610×920 mm ($24 \times 36\frac{1}{8}$ in)
Lent by the Victoria and Albert Museum, London

A later hand than Cockerell's has pencilled on to this drawing 'Portico Front' which would seem to mean that it represents the E range of the courtyard. This can hardly be the case since the sunlight is coming from the left-hand, i.e. N, side. The pencilled alterations on the upper façades of the façade are characteristic of Cockerell's endlessly restive approach to design.

41 CHARLES ROBERT COCKERELL (1788–1863)

Competition design for University Library, Cambridge
Elevation of W side of courtyard
Pencil, partly tinted: 330×470 mm ($13 \times 18\frac{1}{2}$ in)
REPRODUCED: D. J. Watkin, *The Life and Work of C. R. Cockerell, R. A.*, 1974, pl. 90
Lent by the University Library, Cambridge

Another version of this original and powerful façade. Cockerell has now developed the arched chimney-stacks on the skyline which appeared tentatively in no. 40 and which are inspired by Vanbrugh.

42 CHARLES ROBERT COCKERELL (1788–1863)
Competition design for University Library, Cambridge, 1835–6
Elevation of N side of courtyard
Pencil, partly tinted: 455 × 825 mm (18 × 32½ in)
LITERATURE: D. J. Watkin, *The Life and Work of C. R. Cockerell, R.A.*,
    1974, chap. 11, repr. pl. 89
Lent by the Victoria and Albert Museum, London

The design of the lower two storeys corresponds fairly closely with what Cockerell subsequently built on this site. In executing the attic he eliminated the proposed frieze of swags, also the curious centre-piece derived from French Mannerist precedent.

43 CHARLES ROBERT COCKERELL (1788–1863)
Competition design for University Library, Cambridge, 1835–6
Details of window in N side of courtyard
Pencil, partly tinted: 445 × 515 mm (17½ × 20¼ in)
LITERATURE: D. J. Watkin, *The Life and Work of C. R. Cockerell, R.A.*,
    1974, chap. 11
Lent by the Victoria and Albert Museum, London

The mullions with their beautiful pelican heads were unfortunately not executed.

44 CHARLES ROBERT COCKERELL (1788–1863)
Competition design for University Library, Cambridge, 1836
Interior of the Tribune Library
Pencil and wash: 395 × 310 mm (15⅝ × 12⅛ in); insc: The Tribune Library;
    s and d: C.R.C. 13 April 1836
REPRODUCED: D. J. Watkin, *The Life and Work of C. R. Cockerell, R. A.*,
    1974, pl. 94
Lent by the Victoria and Albert Museum, London

40   This drawing was made between the closing date for the third competition (18 February 1836) and the date on which Cockerell's designs were chosen by the Syndicate (11 May 1836). It is not clear what part of the library it represents.

45   CHARLES ROBERT COCKERELL (1788–1863)
Competition design for University Library, Cambridge
Ground-floor plan; view of library interior
Pen, pencil and wash: 420 × 535 mm (16½ × 21 in)
Lent by the Victoria and Albert Museum, London

An apparently contemporary hand (not Cockerell's) has inscribed this drawing 'Cambridge University Library, Hall in place of Quadrangle'. This magnificent conception is for a great two-storeyed library inspired by the Roman Baths.

THE FITZWILLIAM MUSEUM

The competition of 1834–5 for the Fitzwilliam Museum was more smoothly conducted than most in the nineteenth century. It also gave an opportunity for a young architect to provide a distinguished and important building which has been universally admired ever since it was put up. The only point of contention has been the staircase-hall which in its final form represents Basevi's ideas adapted first by C. R. Cockerell and secondly by E. M. Barry. The problem, as Basevi himself was aware, was occasioned by the decision to lend prominence to the portico by placing it on a raised platform high up above street level. This meant that the entrance hall had to contain not merely stairs leading up to the principal galleries but also down to the galleries at street level at the back of the building. The problem of how to combine on the not very large site of the museum all these stairs with a fitting entrance-hall which had also to be used for the display of sculpture, could never be entirely satisfactorily resolved. Basevi's first proposal was for a central staircase descending through a tunnel-like archway flanked by two ascending flights. He subsequently changed his mind so as to turn the central flight into one of ascent and the side flights into descent. Before his sudden death in 1845 he had changed his mind about this yet again but Cockerell, in executing the staircases, adopted a scheme of two ascending staircases flanked by two descending. These were never fully completed and in 1870 it was decided to complete the staircase-hall and at the same time to render it less crowded. M. D. Wyatt's breathtaking solution was not adopted and instead Barry was commissioned to create more space by placing the descending staircases on the sites occupied by the keeper's and porter's offices.

The fine plasterwork of Basevi's ceilings, the bold sculptural details carved by W. G. Nicholl, the sumptuous metal gates and cheveaux-de-frise along the balustraded entrance-wall, are all rich in allusion to Greek and Roman sources and help make the building, like its contents, a liberal education in itself. The Neo-Classical vision of the public museum which gave us Klenze's Glyptothek in Munich of 1816, Schinkel's Altes Museum in Berlin and Smirke's British Museum both of 1823, Wilkins' National Gallery of 1832 and countless other proud porticos in Europe and North America, has found no finer or more eloquent expression than in the Fitzwilliam Museum, this great Temple of the Arts.

46 CHARLES HEATHCOTE TATHAM (1772–1842)
Design for Fitzwilliam Museum, Cambridge, 1827
Elevation of entrance front and plan of principal floor
Pen and watercolour: 350 × 200 mm (13¾ × 8 in)
REPRODUCED: C. Proudfoot & D. Watkin, 'A Pioneer of English Neo-Classicism: C. H. Tatham', *Country Life*, CLI, 1972, 921, fig. 12
PROVENANCE: Fitzwilliam Museum, Cambridge (on loan from the Cambridge Antiquarian Society)

An important though still little-known figure in the history of English Neo-Classicism, Tatham's most characteristic architectural productions were museums and mausolea—those twin constants of the Neo-Classical age. By 1827 he had designed picture galleries at Castle Howard, Yorkshire, Brocklesby Park, Lincolnshire, and Cleveland House, London. Perhaps a friend in Cambridge may have given him the idea of proposing a design for the Fitzwilliam Museum as soon as the site was settled in the 1820s. He is listed amongst those who entered the competition in 1834 but it is not known whether he exhibited this design or a later one now lost. His design of 1827 was ruthless in its acceptance of the fact that top-lit galleries necessarily implied windowless walls. Equally characteristic of Neo-Classical design was the way in which he made his long windowless façade acceptable by recalling an antique source, the Stoa (sometimes called Library of Hadrian) in Athens, a Hellenistic building known from the illustrations in Stuart and Revett's *Antiquities of Athens*, vol. 1, 1762.

Competition design for Fitzwilliam Museum, Cambridge, 1834
Perspective from SE
Pencil and sepia wash: 495 × 690 mm (19½ × 27¼ in)
PROVENANCE: Fitzwilliam Museum, Cambridge

A powerful and original design by a little-known architect who gave as his address, Rectory, St John's Wood, London. The architectural fantasies of J. M. Gandy (1771–1843) may have been a source of inspiration. Hitchcock's ground-floor and first-floor plans also survive in the possession of the museum.

48 J. J. HITCHCOCK

Competition design for Fitzwilliam Museum, Cambridge, 1834
E–W section
Pencil and wash: 498 × 685 mm (19½ × 27 in)
PROVENANCE: Fitzwilliam Museum, Cambridge

This drawing shows that the interior would have been dominated by an impressive, colonnaded, circular hall for the display of sculpture. Its design shows that Hitchcock was anxious to move away from the standard Neo-Classical rotunda inspired by the Pantheon in Rome.

49 HENRY DUESBURY (fl. 1832–1850)

Competition design for Fitzwilliam Museum, Cambridge, 1834
Perspective of the entrance façade
Pen, partly tinted: 475 × 930 mm (18 × 36½ in)
REPRODUCED: *Catalogue of the RIBA Drawings Collection, C–F*, 1972, fig. 66
Lent by the RIBA Drawings Collection

44 The Italianate classicism of this obscure architect has a definitely early-Victorian feel, reminiscent of provincial corn-exchanges and railway stations. It is also anticipatory of Wyatt and Brandon's Assize Courts, Cambridge (1840, dem. 1952).

50 SIR EDWARD CUST (1794–1878) PLATE 13
Design for Fitzwilliam Museum, Cambridge
Elevation of the entrance façade
Pen, pencil and wash with a lined wash border: w/m 1830: 460 × 660 mm (18⅛ × 26 in) insc: A Volunteer Design for the Fitzwilliam Museum with a view to recommend the Italian style of architecture for the new building by Lᵗ Colⁿ the Honble Sir Edward Cust. As this design is not put forward to prejudice the competition – the style (if approved) may be adapted in its general characteristics to whatever plan shall be preferred from amongst those of the competing architects.
PROVENANCE: Fitzwilliam Museum, Cambridge

Sir Edward Cust was an unusual figure, a lieutenant-general and military historian, who was also master of the ceremonies to Queen Victoria and a commissioner for the rebuilding of the Houses of Parliament and for selecting the Wellington monument. Like Duesbury's design for the Fitzwilliam Museum, Cust's anticipates the full-blooded Italianate Revival as typified by the remodelling of Burlington House, Piccadilly, by Banks and Barry in 1868–73. Equally, Cust's implication that his elevation could be made to fit whatever plan might eventually be selected anticipates the confused architectural thinking which Victorian competitions were to engender. Nevertheless, as an early attempt to escape from the Neo-Classical strait-jacket Sir Edward Cust's design is of considerable interest, though the thirty-five smallish windows on the entrance front would have been highly inappropriate as a method of lighting the picture galleries behind.

Competition design for Fitzwilliam Museum, Cambridge, 1834
Elevation of the entrance façade; section
Pen, pencil and wash with a lined wash border, mounted on card:
   535 × 740 mm (21 × 29¼ in); insc: no. 2
PROVENANCE: Fitzwilliam Museum, Cambridge

Six of Vulliamy's competition drawings, mounted on card with tabs for hanging on display, were purchased by the Museum in 1959 (Spencer George Perceval Fund). They are an important addition to our knowledge of a talented, prolific though little-investigated architect. His designs are still in the Greek Revival manner of his Law Institution in Chancery Lane (1830–2) and differ strikingly from his best-known building, Dorchester House, Park Lane (1851–7, dem. 1929), the most magnificent palazzo in England. His Fitzwilliam Museum design is at once novel and Neo-Classical, with its windowless front dominated by a Greek Ionic colonnade, and its surprising rounded ends containing a large lecture-theatre and a sculpture gallery. A huge dome lights the circular library and there are severely functional rectangular lights in the attic storey.

52   LEWIS VULLIAMY (1791–1871)
Competition design for Fitzwilliam Museum, Cambridge, 1834
Plan of the principal floor
Pen and wash with a lined wash border: mounted on card: 530 × 740 mm
   (20⅞ × 29¼ in); insc: no. 2
PROVENANCE: Fitzwilliam Museum, Cambridge

53   LEWIS VULLIAMY (1791–1871)
Competition design for Fitzwilliam Museum, Cambridge, 1834
Elevation of the entrance façade; section (alternative design)

46 Pen, pencil and wash with a lined wash border; mounted on card: 520 ×
745 mm (20$\frac{3}{8}$ × 29$\frac{1}{4}$ in); insc: no. 3
PROVENANCE: Fitzwilliam Museum, Cambridge

Vulliamy's alternative design omits the rounded ends which he may have
felt were too daring to be acceptable. The prominent horizontality of the
long unbroken entablature is characteristically Neo-Classical, as is the
continuous figured frieze and the fourteen statue-filled niches.

54 LEWIS VULLIAMY (1791–1871)
Competition design for Fitzwilliam Museum, Cambridge, 1834
Plan for the alternative design
Pen, pencil and wash with a lined wash border; mounted on card:
525 × 745 mm (20$\frac{5}{8}$ × 29$\frac{1}{4}$ in); insc: no. 3
PROVENANCE: Fitzwilliam Museum, Cambridge

55 THOMAS RICKMAN (1776–1841) and RICHARD
CHARLES HUSSEY   PLATE 15
Competition design for Fitzwilliam Museum, Cambridge, 1834
Perspective of the principal front (Design A with Roman Corinthian
order)
Watercolour, mounted: 470 × 735 mm (18$\frac{1}{2}$ × 29 in); Insc on mount:
Design A no. 8; s and d: Rickman & Hussey Archts. Birmingham
April 1835
LITERATURE: A. James, 'Rickman and the Fitzwilliam Competition',
Architectural Review, CXXI, April 1957, 270–1, repr. 271; J. Cornforth,
'The Fitzwilliam Museum, Cambridge', *Country Life*, CXXXII, 1962,
1278–81, repr. fig. 3; *Catalogue of the RIBA Drawings Collection, O–R*,
1976, p. 142
Lent by the RIBA Drawings Collection

Regarded purely as works of art the watercolours submitted by Rickman and Hussey in the Fitzwilliam Museum competition are of high imaginative quality. Of the three schemes proposed, however, those in the Greek Doric and in the Gothic styles are obviously fantastic considered as architecture. The most sensible and the most attractive is the Roman Corinthian scheme exhibited here in nos. 55–7. Its great open portico is perhaps inspired by Robert Adam's at Osterley Park, Middlesex (1761–80). All the designs were prepared shortly before Hussey assumed command of the partnership in 1835 and it was he who doubtless mounted and 'signed' the drawings in that year; 'The office staff at the time was led by J. A. Bell, who returned from a visit to Rome in 1833. This is perhaps significant in view of the boldness and imagination of these museum designs' (*RIBA Drawings Catalogue, O–R*, 1967, p. 142).

56   THOMAS RICKMAN (1776–1841) and RICHARD CHARLES HUSSEY   PLATE 16

Competition design for Fitzwilliam Museum, Cambridge, 1834
View within the court (Design A with Roman Corinthian order)
Watercolour, mounted: 305×490 mm ($12 \times 19\frac{1}{4}$ in); insc on mount:
  Design A no. 9; s and d: as for no. 55
LITERATURE: As for no. 55
Lent by the RIBA Drawings Collection

57   THOMAS RICKMAN (1776–1841) and RICHARD CHARLES HUSSEY

Competition design for Fitzwilliam Museum, Cambridge, 1834
Interior of library (Design A with Roman Corinthian order)
Watercolour, mounted: 330×235 mm ($13 \times 9\frac{1}{4}$ in); insc on mount:
  Design A no. 10; s and d: as for no. 55
LITERATURE: As for no. 55
Lent by the RIBA Drawings Collection

58 THOMAS RICKMAN (1776–1841) and RICHARD
    CHARLES HUSSEY   PLATE 17
Competition design for Fitzwilliam Museum, Cambridge, 1834
Perspective of the front elevation (Design C with Greek Doric order)
Watercolour, mounted: 470 × 755 mm (18½ × 30½ in); insc on mount:
    Design C no. 8; s and d: as for no. 55
LITERATURE: As for no. 55
Lent by the RIBA Drawings Collection

This grandiose classical design with a Roman rotunda rising incongruously above Greek porticos is ultimately inspired by Ledoux's Barrière de
la Villette, Paris (1783). The anti-Baroque device of the domeless drum
is typically Neo-Classical and is also French in origin, deriving from
Le Pautre.

59 THOMAS RICKMAN (1776–1841) and RICHARD
    CHARLES HUSSEY   PLATE 18
Competition design for Fitzwilliam Museum, Cambridge, 1834
Interior of library; interior of lower front gallery; interior of upper
    front gallery (Design C with Greek Doric order)
Watercolour: 165 × 335 mm (6½ × 13¼ in); pen: 125 × 205 mm (5 × 8 in),
    140 × 210 mm (5½ × 8¼ in); the three drawings mounted together; insc
    on mount: Design C no. 9; s and d: as for no. 55
LITERATURE: As for no. 55
Lent by the RIBA Drawings Collection

60 THOMAS RICKMAN (1776–1841) and RICHARD
    CHARLES HUSSEY   PLATE 19
Competition design for Fitzwilliam Museum, Cambridge, 1834
Perspective of the front elevation (Design B in Decorated Gothic)
Watercolour, mounted: 745 × 520 mm (29⅜ × 20½ in); insc: Design B
    no. 6; s and d: as for no. 55

LITERATURE: As for no. 55; and see *Victoria History of the Counties of England, Cambridgeshire and the Isle of Ely*, vol. 3, 1959, repr. facing p. 388 from a copy at the Fitzwilliam Museum
Lent by the RIBA Drawings Collection

Yet more fantastic than the classical design inspired by Ledoux, this spectacular *tour de force* looks back to James Wyatt's improbable Fonthill Abbey, Wiltshire (1796–1807), for William Beckford.

61 THOMAS RICKMAN (1776–1841) **and RICHARD CHARLES HUSSEY**   PLATE 20
Competition design for Fitzwilliam Museum, Cambridge, 1834
Interior of library; view of the grand staircase (Design B in Decorated Gothic)
Watercolour, mounted: 295 × 210 mm (11⅝ × 8¼ in), 270 × 160 mm (10⅝ × 6¼ in); insc: Design B nos. 7 & 8; s and d: as for no. 55
LITERATURE: As for no. 55
Lent by the RIBA Drawings Collection

Rickman and Hussey have now been entirely overtaken by fantasy in their ecclesiastical-looking library with not a single book to be seen and in their wild sinuous staircase which would surely have been the principal exhibit in the museum.

62 GEORGE BASEVI (1794–1845)   PLATE 21
Competition design for Fitzwilliam Museum, Cambridge, 1834
Ground-floor plan
Pen, partly tinted, with a lined wash border: 540 × 840 mm (21⅜ × 33 in); insc: no. 1
PROVENANCE: Fitzwilliam Museum, Cambridge

This is one of Basevi's original competition designs and, like the eight following drawings, is mounted on card with tabs for hanging on display. It shows that Basevi's first idea was to use the three ground-floor rooms at the back of the building as an extended library.

63 GEORGE BASEVI (1794–1845)
Competition design for Fitzwilliam Museum, Cambridge, 1834
First-floor plan
Pen, partly tinted, with a lined wash border: 545 × 840 mm ($21\frac{3}{8}$ × 33 in);
  insc: no. 2
PROVENANCE: Fitzwilliam Museum, Cambridge

64 GEORGE BASEVI (1794–1845)   PLATE 22
Competition design for Fitzwilliam Museum, Cambridge, 1834
Elevation of principal front
Pen, partly tinted, with a lined wash border: 545 × 845 mm ($21\frac{1}{2}$ × $33\frac{1}{4}$ in);
  insc: no. 3
PROVENANCE: Fitzwilliam Museum, Cambridge

65 GEORGE BASEVI (1794–1845)
Competition design for Fitzwilliam Museum, Cambridge, 1834
Elevation of W front
Pen, partly tinted; 530 × 900 mm ($20\frac{7}{8}$ × $35\frac{3}{8}$ in); insc: no. 4
PROVENANCE: Fitzwilliam Museum, Cambridge

This shows the round-headed windows which Basevi was to alter to a pedimented form in execution. The long garlands between the pilasters were eliminated in the contract drawings.

66 GEORGE BASEVI (1794–1845)
Competition design for Fitzwilliam Museum, Cambridge, 1834
Elevation of S front
Pen, partly tinted: 535 × 900 mm (21 × 35½ in); insc: no. 5
PROVENANCE: Fitzwilliam Museum, Cambridge

67 GEORGE BASEVI (1794–1845)
Competition design for Fitzwilliam Museum, Cambridge, 1834
Section from E to W
Pen, partly tinted, with a lined wash border: 545 × 840 mm (21⅜ × 33 in);
  insc: no. 6
PROVENANCE: Fitzwilliam Museum, Cambridge

Basevi's conception of the entrance hall was rooted in Greek Revival
practice as is made clear in his specification that the frieze should be cast
from that at the Temple of Apollo Epicurius at Bassae, and the caryatids
flanking the first-floor doorways from the Sanctuary of Pandrosus (i.e.
the Erectheion in Athens). The caryatid-flanked doorways were not
executed in Basevi's lifetime and the Bassae frieze was removed by
E. M. Barry. However, Barry did execute the central doorway on the
first floor from Basevi's designs in 1874.

68 GEORGE BASEVI (1794–1845)
Competition design for Fitzwilliam Museum, Cambridge, 1834
Longitudinal section from S to N
Pen, partly tinted, with a lined wash border: 545 × 840 mm (21½ × 33 in);
  insc: no. 7
PROVENANCE: Fitzwilliam Museum, Cambridge

The cast of the Parthenon frieze in the principal gallery was bought from
the Trustees of the British Museum in 1837. It still survives though the
lower parts of the room were altered during the Directorship of Sir
Sidney Cockerell.

52 69 GEORGE BASEVI (1794–1845)

Competition designs for Fitzwilliam Museum, Cambridge, 1834
View of one of the small galleries; view of the principal gallery; view
    from library entrance looking up to principal entrance
Pencil: 530 × 840 mm (20⅞ × 33 in); insc: no. 9
PROVENANCE: Fitzwilliam Museum, Cambridge

These drawings give one a clear impression of the crowded practice of
picture hanging which had survived from the Baroque period into the
age of Neo-Classicism.

70 GEORGE BASEVI (1794–1845)   PLATE 24

Competition designs for Fitzwilliam Museum, Cambridge, 1834
Staircase-hall looking W; perspective view of staircase-hall from N
    landing
Pen and sepia wash with lined wash border: 545 × 860 mm (21½ × 33¾ in);
    insc: no. 8
PROVENANCE: Fitzwilliam Museum, Cambridge

71 GEORGE BASEVI (1794–1845)

Fitzwilliam Museum, Cambridge
Elevation of S front
Pen and wash with ruled border: w/m 1842: 540 × 810 mm (21¼ × 32 in)
PROVENANCE: Fitzwilliam Museum, Cambridge

This and no. 72 show the museum as executed.

72 GEORGE BASEVI (1794–1845)   PLATE 23

Fitzwilliam Museum, Cambridge
Elevation of W front
Pen and wash with ruled border: w/m 1842: 540 × 840 mm (21¼ × 33 in)
PROVENANCE: Fitzwilliam Museum, Cambridge

73 GEORGE BASEVI (1794–1845)

Fitzwilliam Museum, Cambridge

Plan and sections of iron girders and columns in the hall

Pen, partly tinted: 595 × 875 mm (23½ × 34½ in); insc: no. 18

PROVENANCE: Fitzwilliam Museum, Cambridge

This working-drawing reminds one of the extensive use of cast-iron construction which frequently lay behind the masonry and plaster-work of late Neo-Classical buildings. The pioneer of this method of construction was Sir Robert Smirke (for example at the British Museum from 1823 onwards). In fact the four columns in the Fitzwilliam staircase-hall, one of which appears on the left in this drawing, were not executed until after Basevi's death when Cockerell substituted solid monoliths of pink granite for the iron core surrounded by scagliola which Basevi had intended.

74 GEORGE BASEVI (1794–1845)

Fitzwilliam Museum, Cambridge

Plan and sections of construction of upper part of the ends of the façades and side colonnades

Pen, partly tinted: w/m 1835: 605 × 875 mm (23¾ × 34½ in); insc: no. 30

PROVENANCE: Fitzwilliam Museum, Cambridge

Basevi's many working-drawings for the museum show the meticulously detailed information which he gave to craftsmen.

75 GEORGE BASEVI (1794–1845)

Fitzwilliam Museum, Cambridge

Sections through the dome rooms at the S and N ends of the principal gallery

Pen, partly tinted: 545 × 760 mm (21½ × 30 in); insc: no. 88

PROVENANCE: Fitzwilliam Museum, Cambridge

Resembling centrally planned Renaissance chapels, the dome rooms demonstrate the essentially cumulative nature of Neo-Classical design which drew on Greek, Roman and Renaissance sources.

76 GEORGE BASEVI (1794–1845)

Fitzwilliam Museum, Cambridge
Plan, elevation, section and full-size details of centre door into principal
   gallery viewed from the gallery
Pen and wash: 560 × 770 mm (22 × 30¼ in); insc: no. 92
PROVENANCE: Fitzwilliam Museum, Cambridge

This drawing has been selected for exhibition because the doorway, though executed in this form, was replaced when the principal gallery was remodelled in 1932. Doorways of a similar though simplified design survive in the dome rooms and adjacent N and S galleries. The drawing also exemplifies Basevi's careful attention to polychromatic effect and proves that the black, gold and dull-red colouring in the first-floor galleries is due to Basevi and not to later nineteenth-century architects. As early as 1819 Basevi had been deeply impressed by ancient Greek polychromy and wrote in a letter to his master Soane: 'To convey to you an idea of the colouring of Greece is impossible... The effect of painting and gilding the ornaments, the bas-reliefs and statues must have been exquisite, the ancients seem to have left nothing unpainted.' Basevi notes on the drawing that the Ionic order is to be the same as at the Conservative Club, St James's Street, London, which he designed in 1842–3 in collaboration with Sidney Smirke.

77 CHARLES ROBERT COCKERELL (1788–1863)

Designs for Fitzwilliam Museum, Cambridge, 1846–7
Four sketches for staircase-hall

Pencil, mounted on a single sheet in Cockerell's office: 370 × 560 mm
    (14½ × 22 in)
PROVENANCE: Fitzwilliam Museum, Cambridge

These sketches are important for establishing that the essentially
Baroque way in which the drum of the dome over the staircase-hall is
flanked with herms is due to Cockerell and not, as is generally supposed,
to E. M. Barry. Unfortunately few of Cockerell's and none of Barry's
drawings can now be found. In 1870, however, Cockerell's son lent
M. D. Wyatt what the latter described as 'nearly seventy...drawings
and sketches of the highest artistic and architectural merit...for various
portions of the Hall in the hand of C. R. Cockerell'.

78   CHARLES ROBERT COCKERELL (1788–1863)
Design for Fitzwilliam Museum, Cambridge, 1847
Design for painted-glass lunette in staircase-hall
Pen and water-colour: 320 × 490 mm (12⅝ × 19⅜ in); d: 25 October 1847
PROVENANCE: Fitzwilliam Museum, Cambridge

This glass was probably not executed. Cockerell's lunettes lighting the
first-floor landings in the staircase-hall were enlarged by E. M. Barry.

79   MATTHEW DIGBY WYATT (1820–1877)
Design for Fitzwilliam Museum, Cambridge, 1870
Section of ground-floor corridor showing addition of glazed openings in
    the groin vaults at either end to provide extra light; plan of staircase-
    hall as then existing showing proposed addition of entrance apse
Pencil, partly tinted: 550 × 750 mm (21⅝ × 29½ in); insc: no. 2; s and d:
    MDW 1870
PROVENANCE: Fitzwilliam Museum, Cambridge

56 This design and nos. 80 and 81 show M. D. Wyatt's handsome and imaginative solution to the problems posed by the staircase-hall which had been left uncompleted when funds ran out in 1847. It was not surprising that the museum authorities should seek advice from Wyatt since he had been elected the first Slade Professor of Fine Art at Cambridge in 1869, had been one of the father-figures of the Great Exhibition and in 1865 had designed Addenbrooke's Hospital in Cambridge. In the report which he submitted on 10 June 1870 to the 'Syndicate for the rearrangement of the Fitzwilliam Museum', he claimed that 'The Hall of the Fitzwilliam Museum, with the Portico leading to it, is, although incomplete, one of the noblest pieces of Architecture in this Country.' At the same time he pointed out that it represented 'by far the most difficult problem I have ever met with in my professional life'.

There were basically two problems: (1) that the central staircase descending to the ground-floor galleries along the W front contradicted the logic of the ascent to the staircase-hall from pavement level; (2) that the two staircases ascending to the first-floor galleries were so close to the front entrance (i.e. only 10 feet 9 inches away), that the eye could not take in at once both their grandeur and the grandeur of the room as a whole. Wyatt decided not to attempt a solution of problem number (1) since this would involve replacing Cockerell's staircases of which he wrote: 'the more attention I have given to the subject the more I have been led to admire the skill and ingenuity with which Cockerell improved upon Basevi's original conceptions.' Wyatt therefore concentrated upon a solution of problem number (2) which he achieved by creating a coffered entrance apse which would extend the staircase-hall into part of the area occupied by the portico. This would not only be a dramatic feature in itself but would separate by nearly 21 feet the entrance to the museum from Cockerell's staircases of ascent to the principal galleries.

Bold in its unexpected enlargement of the space occupied by the staircase-hall, yet conservative in its retention of Cockerell's work, Wyatt's scheme did not find favour with the Syndicate. Instead, E. M.

Barry (1830–1880) was appointed to complete the staircase-hall, an
architect who had no special gifts to recommend him other than being
the son of a famous architect. Unlike Wyatt, he decided to solve problem (1) not problem (2) even though this involved sweeping away
Cockerell's staircases. His ingenious solution was to replace Cockerell's
central descending staircase with a pair of descending staircases on the
sites formerly occupied by the Keeper's and porter's offices on either
side of the entrance hall. The visitor would not, of course, see these
staircases on entering the building and would not, therefore, feel that
his climb from the street had been worthless. The open floor-space thus
created between the two ascending flights would constitute an additional
visual advantage.

80 MATTHEW DIGBY WYATT (1820–1877)

Design for Fitzwilliam Museum, Cambridge, 1870
Longitudinal section through staircase-hall from E to W
Pencil and wash: 450 × 540 mm (17¾ × 21¼ in); insc: no. 3; s and d; as
   for no. 79
PROVENANCE: Fitzwilliam Museum, Cambridge

This attractive drawing is of interest for showing us not only Wyatt's
proposed apsed addition to the staircase-hall, but also what Cockerell's
treatment of the interior looked like in 1870 (or, at any rate, how Wyatt
interpreted Cockerell's intentions). The drawing shows that the arrangement of the whole ceiling as it exists today is evidently Cockerell's,
including the cove to the central dome and the balustrade surrounding
it. Wyatt does not show the herms in the drum but these, as we have
seen, were anticipated in sketches by Cockerell. Wyatt's letter to the
Syndicate of 1870 states that what was now principally necessary to
complete the staircase-hall was, apparently in order of importance: (1)
a marble pavement; (2) wall-facings; (3) the completion of the first-floor
niches; (4) the balustrading of the staircases; (5) the balustrading bet-

ween the columns on the first-floor landing; (6) marble statues to fill the niches, either copies of antique statues or modern sculpture 'by the best artists' such as Thomas Woolner, J. H. Foley or Patrick McDowell; and (7) a pair of bronze doors. All these, he thought, could be provided for £16,000.

81 MATTHEW DIGBY WYATT (1820–1877)   PLATE 25
Design for Fitzwilliam Museum, Cambridge, 1870
Perspective of proposed new entrance apse in staircase-hall, looking E
Pencil and wash: 465 × 650 mm (18¼ × 25½ in); insc: no. 6; s and d: as
   for no. 79
PROVENANCE: Fitzwilliam Museum, Cambridge

THE MUSEUM OF CLASSICAL ARCHAEOLOGY

The collection of casts of antique sculpture and architecture which is housed today in the Museum of Classical Archaeology in Little St Mary's Lane originated in 1850 with a gift of casts from John Kirkpatrick of Trinity College. The collection grew rapidly and in 1878 the Fitzwilliam Museum Syndicate considered extending the museum to north and south so as to provide galleries for ancient art and especially for casts. The decision in 1879 that art and archaeology should form a special section of the Classical Tripos lent greater urgency to the question of an appropriate gallery and in 1882 a piece of land west of Little St Mary's churchyard was obtained from Peterhouse. In 1883 the malt-houses which occupied this site were skilfully converted into excellent galleries by the architect Basil Champneys and the new building was opened on 6 May 1884.

82 Design for Museum of Classical Archaeology adjacent to Fitzwilliam Museum. Model, *c.* 1878
Wood: 1080 × 1910 × 525 mm (42½ × 75¼ × 20¾ in)
PROVENANCE: Fitzwilliam Museum, Cambridge

The moving spirit behind the museum was Sidney Colvin, Director of the Fitzwilliam Museum and Slade Professor of Fine Art. This model for a new museum immediately S of the Fitzwilliam Museum probably reflects his ideas. The contrast in scale between the two buildings is painful. The apsed E end of the Museum of Classical Archaeology with its engaged Ionic order is derived from the N end of Harvey Lonsdale Elmes's celebrated St George's Hall, Liverpool (1840).

BUSTS

83 EDWARD HODGES BAILY (1788–1867)   PLATE 26
Bust of William Wilkins, 1830
Marble: height 610 mm (24 in); s and d: E. H. BAILY, R.A. Sculp.
London 1830
PROVENANCE: Fitzwilliam Museum, Cambridge (on loan from the
Master and Fellows, Trinity College, Cambridge)

84 ANON.
Bust of George Basevi (1794–1845)
Plaster-cast: height 735 mm (29 in)
PROVENANCE: Fitzwilliam Museum, Cambridge

PLATE 1. William Wilkins: Proposed Porter's Lodge,
Downing College, *c.* 1806

PLATE 2. Lewis William Wyatt: Elevation of S front,
Downing College, 1805

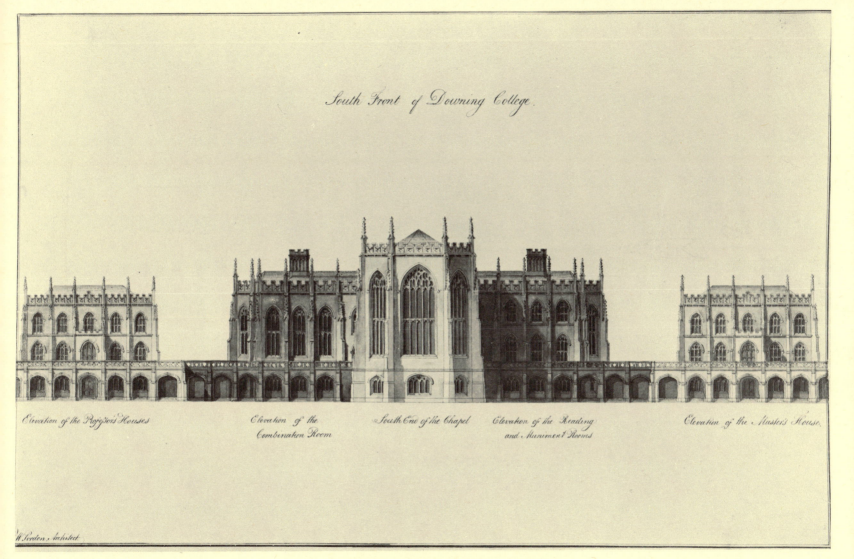

South Front of Downing College.

Elevation of the Professor's Houses   Elevation of the Combination Room   South End of the Chapel   Elevation of the Reading and Muniment Rooms   Elevation of the Master's House.

W. Porden, Architect

PLATE 3. William Porden: Elevation of S front,
Downing College, 1805

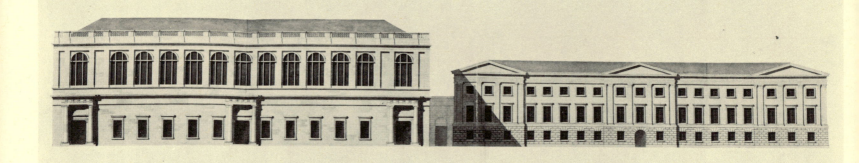

PLATE 4. William Wilkins: Elevation of W front, New Court,
Trinity College, 1821

PLATE 5. View of Cambridge from the Observatory, *c.* 1823

PLATE 6. Edward Lapidge: Perspective of court looking S,
King's College, 1822

PLATE 7. Thomas Rickman and Henry Hutchinson: Perspective
of University Library, Cambridge, from the SE (Design A), 1829

PLATE 8. Thomas Rickman and Henry Hutchinson: Perspective
of University Library, Cambridge, from the SE (Design B), 1829

PLATE 9. William Wilkins: Perspective of University Library,
Cambridge, from the SE, 1830

PLATE 10. Charles Robert Cockerell: Elevation of W side of court,
University Library, Cambridge, *c*. 1835

PLATE 11. Charles Robert Cockerell: Interior of University
Library, Cambridge, 1830

PLATE 12. J. J. Hitchcock: Perspective of Fitzwilliam Museum
from the SE, 1834

A VOLVNTEER DESIGN FOR THE FITZWILLIAM MVSEVM.

WITH A VIEW TO RECOMMEND THE ITALIAN STYLE OF ARCHITECTVRE FOR THE NEW BVILDING.

BY LT COLL THE HONBLE SIR EDWARD CUST.

AS THIS DESIGN IS NOT PVT FORWARD TO PREJVDICE THE COMPETITION – NO PLAN ACCOMPANIES THIS ELEVATION,

THE STYLE IF APPROVED OF MAY BE ADAPTED IN ITS GENERAL CHARACTERISTICS TO WHATEVER PLAN SHALL BE PREFERRED FROM AMONG THOSE OF THE COMPETING ARCHITECTS.

PLATE 13. Sir Edward Cust: Elevation of E front,
Fitzwilliam Museum, c. 1834

Elevation of a Design for the Fitzwilliam Museum

PLATE 14. Lewis Vulliamy: Elevation of E front,
Fitzwilliam Museum, 1834

PLATE 15. Thomas Rickman and Richard Charles Hussey: Perspective
of Fitzwilliam Museum from the SE (Design A), 1834

PLATE 16. Thomas Rickman and Richard Charles Hussey: View
within the court, Fitzwilliam Museum (Design A), 1834

PLATE 17. Thomas Rickman and Richard Charles Hussey: Perspective
of Fitzwilliam Museum from the SE (Design C), 1834

PLATE 18. Thomas Rickman and Richard Charles Hussey: Interior
views of Fitzwilliam Museum (Design C), 1834

PLATE 19. Thomas Rickman and Richard Charles Hussey: Perspective
of Fitzwilliam Museum from the SE (Design B), 1834

PLATE 20. Thomas Rickman and Richard Charles Hussey:
Interior views of Fitzwilliam Museum (Design B), 1834

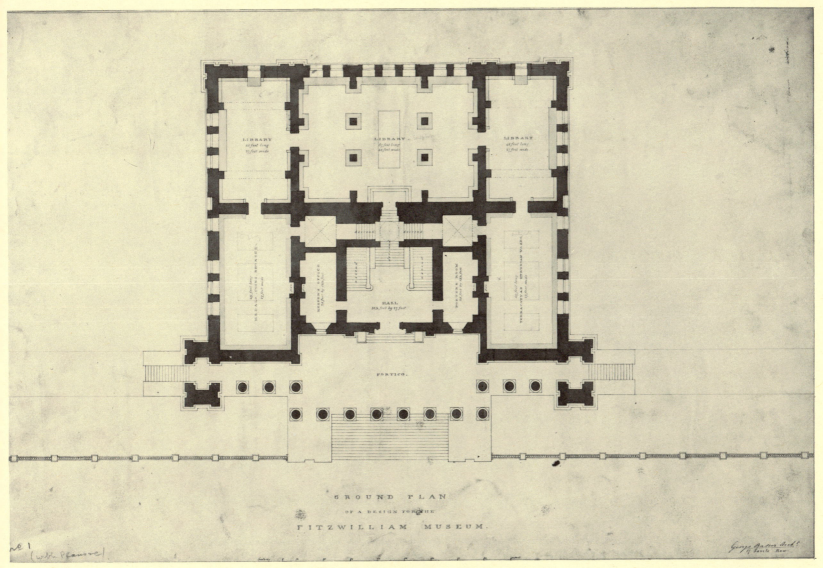

GROUND PLAN

OF A DESIGN FOR THE

FITZWILLIAM MUSEUM.

PLATE 21. George Basevi: Ground-floor plan of
Fitzwilliam Museum, 1834

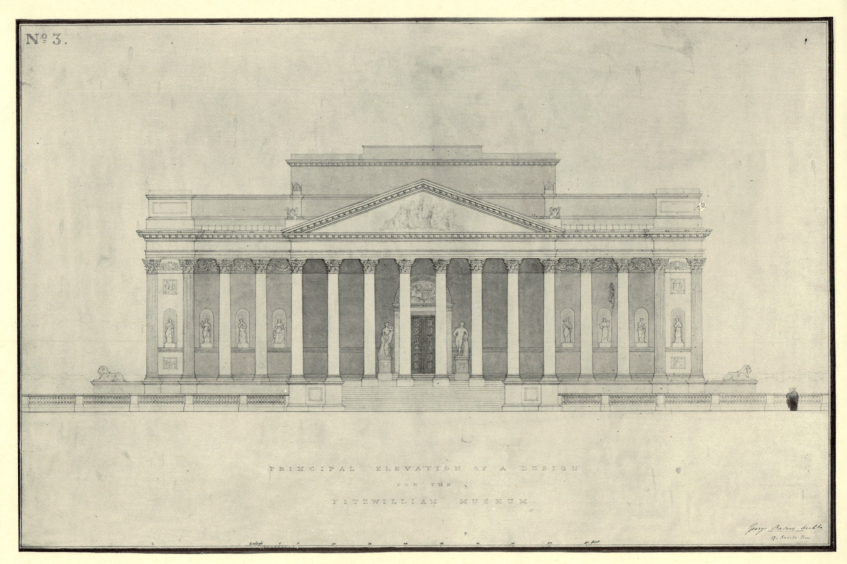

PRINCIPAL ELEVATION OF A DESIGN
FOR THE
FITZWILLIAM MUSEUM.

PLATE 22. George Basevi: Elevation of E front,
Fitzwilliam Museum, 1834

Back Elevation (with roof)
with Plans etc

PLATE 23. George Basevi: Elevation of W front,
Fitzwilliam Museum, 1834

PLATE 24. George Basevi: Interior views of Fitzwilliam
Museum, 1834

FITZWILLIAM MUSEUM.

Sketch showing the proposed
enlargement of hall.

PLATE 25. Matthew Digby Wyatt: Perspective looking E
of proposed entrance apse in staircase-hall, Fitzwilliam
Museum, 1870

PLATE 26. Edward Hodges Baily: Bust of William Wilkins, 1830